Flesh and Blood

C.K. Williams

Farrar / Straus / Giroux

New York

FLESH AND BLOOD

Library of Congress Cataloging-in-Publication Data
Williams, C. K. (Charles Kenneth).
Flesh and blood.
I. Title.
PS3573.I4483F5   1987   811'.54   87-7391

Acknowledgments are made to *The American Poetry Review, The
Atlantic, The Berkeley Review, Cross Currents, Ironwood, The
Missouri Review, New England Review/Breadloaf Quarterly,
The Ontario Review, Open Places, The Paris Review, Pequod,
Seneca Review, Sulphur, Tri-Quarterly,* and *A
Celebration for Stanley Kunitz,* where some of these poems
originally appeared. "Travelers," "Girl Meets Boy," "Love:
Intimacy," "Hooks," "Philadelphia: 1978," "Self-knowledge,"
"Rungs," "Drought," and "Guatemala: 1964" were first
published in *Antaeus.* "First Desires," "Love: Beginnings," and
"Love: Habit" originally appeared in *The New Yorker.*
"Religious Thought," "Anger," "Blame," and "New Car" were
first published in *Ploughshares*

A good number of the poems were finished with the help of a
grant from the National Endowment for the Arts.

For my father,
Paul B. Williams

Contents

I

II

III

I

Elms

All morning the tree men have been taking down the stricken elms skirt-
   ing the broad sidewalks.
The pitiless electric chain saws whine tirelessly up and down their pierc-
   ing, operatic scales
and the diesel choppers in the street shredding the debris chug feverishly,
   incessantly,
packing truckload after truckload with the feathery, homogenized, inert
   remains of heartwood,
twig and leaf and soon the block is stripped, it is as though illusions of
   reality were stripped:
the rows of naked facing buildings stare and think, their divagations more
   urgent than they were.
"The winds of time," they think, the mystery charged with fearful clarity:
   "The winds of time . . ."
All afternoon, on to the unhealing evening, minds racing, "Insolent, uncon-
   scionable, the winds of time . . ."

Hooks

Possibly because she's already so striking—tall, well dressed, very clear,
   pure skin—
when the girl gets on the subway at Lafayette Street everyone notices her
   artificial hand
but we also manage, as we almost always do, not to be noticed noticing,
   except one sleeping woman,
who hasn't budged since Brooklyn but who lifts her head now, opens up,
   forgets herself,
and frankly stares at those intimidating twists of steel, the homely leather
   sock and laces,
so that the girl, as she comes through the door, has to do in turn now what
   is to be done,
which is to look down at it, too, a bit askance, with an air of tolerant, be-
   mused annoyance,
the way someone would glance at their unruly, apparently ferocious but
   really quite friendly dog.

Nostalgia

In the dumbest movie they can play it on us with a sunrise and a passage
of adagio Vivaldi—
all the reason more to love it and to loathe it, this always barely choked-
back luscious flood,
this turbulence in breast and breath that indicates a purity residing some-
where in us,
redeeming with its easy access the thousand lapses of memory shed in the
most innocuous day
and canceling our rue for all the greater consciousness we didn't have for
past, lost presents.
Its illusion is that we'll retain this new, however hammy past more thor-
oughly than all before,
its reality, that though we know by heart its shabby ruses, know we'll mis-
place it yet again,
it's what we have, a stage light flickering to flood, chintz and gaud, and we
don't care.

Artemis

The lesbian couple's lovely toddler daughter has one pierced ear with a
thin gold ring in it
and the same abundant, flaming, almost movie-starlet hair as the chunkier
of the women.
For an entire hour she has been busily harrying the hapless pigeons of the
Parc Montholon
while the other two sit spooning on a bench, caressing, cradling one an-
other in their arms
then striking up acquaintance with a younger girl who at last gets up to
leave with them.
They call the child but she doesn't want to go just yet, she's still in the
game she's made.
It's where you creep up softly on your quarry, then shriek and stamp and
run and wave your arms
and watch as it goes waddle, waddle, waddle, and heaves itself to your
great glee into the air.

4 /

Guatemala: 1964

for Loren Crabtree

The Maya-Quechua Indians plodding to market on feet as flat and tough
    as toads were semi-starving
but we managed to notice only their brilliant weaving and implacable,
    picturesque aloofness.
The only people who would talk to us were the village alcoholic, who sold
    his soul for *aguardiente*,
and the Bahia nurse, Jenny, middle-aged, English-Nicaraguan, the sole
    medicine for eighty miles,
who lord knows why befriended us, put us up, even took us in her jeep
    into the mountains,
where a child, if I remember, needed penicillin, and where the groups of
    dark, idling men
who since have risen and been crushed noted us with something discon-
    certingly beyond suspicion.
Good Jenny: it took this long to understand she wasn't just forgiving our
    ferocious innocence.

Herakles

A mysterious didactic urgency informs the compelling bedtime stories he
    is obsessively recounted.
Misty, potent creatures, half human, half insane with hatred and with lust-
    ings for the hearth:
the childhood of the race, with always, as the ground, the urgent implica-
    tion of a lesson.
Some of it he gets, that there are losses, personal and epic, but bearable,
    to be withstood,
and that the hero's soul is self-forged, self-conceived, hammered out in
    outrage, trial, abandon, risk.
The parables elude him, though: he can never quite grasp where the ever-
    after means to manifest.
Is he supposed to *be* this darkly tempered, dark fanatic of the flesh who'll
    surely consume himself?
Or should it be the opposite: would all these feats and deeds be not ex-
    emplary but cautionary?

First Desires

It was like listening to the record of a symphony before you knew anything
  at all about the music,
what the instruments might sound like, look like, what portion of the or-
  chestra each represented:
there were only volumes and velocities, thickenings and thinnings, the
  winding cries of change
that seemed to touch within you, through your body, to be part of you and
  then apart from you.
And even when you'd learned the grainy timbre of the single violin, the
  ardent arpeggios of the horn,
when you tried again there were still uneases and confusions left, an ache,
  a sense of longing
that held you in chromatic dissonance, droning on beyond the dominant's
  resolve into the tonic,
as though there were a flaw of logic in the structure, or in (you knew it
  was more likely) you.

The Dirty Talker: D Line, Boston

Shabby, tweedy, academic, he was old enough to be her father and I
  thought he was her father,
then realized he was standing closer than a father would so I thought he
  was her older lover.
And I thought at first that she was laughing, then saw it was more serious,
  more strenuous:
her shoulders spasmed back and forth; he was leaning close, his mouth
  almost against her ear.
He's terminating the affair, I thought: wife ill, the kids . . . the girl won't
  let him go.
We were in a station now, he pulled back half a head from her the better
  to behold her,
then was out the hissing doors, she sobbing wholly now so that finally I
  had to understand—
her tears, his grinning broadly in—at *me* now though, as though I were a
  portion of the story.

Repression

More and more lately, as, not even minding the slippages yet, the aches
and sad softenings,
I settle into my other years, I notice how many of what I once thought
were evidences of repression,
sexual or otherwise, now seem, in other people anyway, to be varieties of
dignity, withholding, tact,
and sometimes even in myself, certain patiences I would have once called
lassitude, indifference,
now seem possibly to be if not the rewards then at least the unsuspected,
undreamed-of conclusions
to many of the even-then-preposterous self-evolved disciplines, rigors, al-
most mortifications
I inflicted on myself in my starting-out days, improvement days, days
when the idea alone of psychic peace,
of intellectual, of emotional quiet, the merest hint, would have meant in-
conceivable capitulation.

Como

In the Mercedes station wagon with diplomatic plates the mother has gone
out somewhere again.
The husband is who knows and who cares where in his silver Porsche
nine-twenty-eight.
As they come across the dismal hotel garden from their after-dinner prom-
enade along the lake,
the three noisy, bratty kids are all over the pretty German teenager who
minds them.
One tugs at one hand, another at the other, the snotty baby pulls at her
wrinkled skirt and wails
but for all the *au pair* notices they might not be there, she might be on the
dance floor at a ball.
It's not until the grizzled kitchen mouse-cat strolls out on the path that she
comes to life,
kneeling, whispering, fervently coaxing the coy thing with tempting clicks
and rubbings of her hands.

One Morning in Brooklyn

The snow is falling in three directions at once against the sienna brick of
     the houses across,
but the storm is mild, the light even, the erratic wind not harsh, and, toll-
     ing ten o'clock,
the usually undistinguished bells of the Sixth Street cathedral assume an
     authoritative dignity,
remarking with ponderous self-consciousness the holy singularities of this
     now uncommon day.
How much the pleasant sense, in our sheltering rooms, of warmth, enclo-
     sure: an idle, languid taking in,
with almost Georgian ease, voluptuous, reposeful, including titillations of
     the sin of well-being,
the gentle adolescent tempest, which still can't make up its mind quite,
     can't dig in and bite,
everything for show, flailing with a furious but futile animation wisps of
     white across the white.

Self-knowledge

Because he was always the good-hearted one, the ingenuous one, the one
     who knew no cunning,
who, if "innocent" didn't quite apply, still merited some similar connota-
     tion of naïveté, simplicity,
the sense that an essential awareness of the coarseness of other people's
     motives was lacking
so that he was constantly blundering upon situations in which he would
     take on good faith
what the other rapaciously, ruthlessly, duplicitously and nearly always
     successfully offered as truth . . .
All of that he understood about himself but he was also aware that he
     couldn't alter at all
his basic affable faith in the benevolence of everyone's intentions and that
     because of this the world
would not as in romance annihilate him but would toy unmercifully with
     him until he was mad.

Alzheimer's: The Wife

for Renée Mauger

She answers the bothersome telephone, takes the message, forgets the message, forgets who called.

One of their daughters, her husband guesses: the one with the dogs, the babies, the boy Jed?

Yes, perhaps, but how tell which, how tell anything when all the name tags have been lost or switched,

when all the lonely flowers of sense and memory bloom and die now in adjacent bites of time?

Sometimes her own face will suddenly appear with terrifying inappropriateness before her in a mirror.

She knows that if she's patient, its gaze will break, demurely, decorously, like a well-taught child's,

it will turn from her as though it were embarrassed by the secrets of this awful hide-and-seek.

If she forgets, though, and glances back again, it will still be in there, furtively watching, crying.

Alzheimer's: The Husband

for Jean Mauger

He'd been a clod, he knew, yes, always aiming toward his vision of the good life, always acting on it.

He knew he'd been unconscionably self-centered, had indulged himself with his undreamed-of good fortune,

but he also knew that the single-mindedness with which he'd attended to his passions, needs and whims,

and which must have seemed to others the grossest sort of egotism, was also what was really at the base

of how he'd almost offhandedly worked out the intuitions and moves which had brought him here,

and this wasn't all that different: to spend his long anticipated retirement learning to cook,

clean house, dress her, even to apply her makeup, wasn't any sort of secular saintliness—

that would be belittling—it was just the next necessity he saw himself as being called to.

The Critic

In the Boston Public Library on Boylston Street, where all the bums come
    in stinking from the cold,
there was one who had a battered loose-leaf book he used to scribble in
    for hours on end.
He wrote with no apparent hesitation, quickly, and with concentration;
    his inspiration was inspiring:
you had to look again to realize that he was writing over words that were
    already there—
blocks of cursive etched into the softened paper, interspersed with poems
    in print he'd pasted in.
I hated to think of the volumes he'd violated to construct his opus, but I
    liked him anyway,
especially the way he'd often reach the end, close his work with weary
    satisfaction, then open again
and start again: page one, chapter one, his blood-rimmed eyes as rapt as
    David's doing psalms.

New Car

Doesn't, when we touch it, that sheen of infinitesimally pebbled steel,
    doesn't it, perhaps,
give just a bit, yes, the subtlest yielding, yes, much less than flesh would,
    we realize,
but still, as though it were intending in some formal way that at last we
    were to be in contact
with the world of inorganics, as though, after all we've been through with
    it, cuts, falls, blows,
that world, the realm of carbon, iron, earth, the all-ungiving, was attempt-
    ing, gently, patiently,
to reach across, respond, and mightn't we find now, not to our horror or
    even our discomfort,
that our tongue, as though in answer, had wandered gently from the
    mouth, as though it, too,
shriven of its limits, bud and duct, would sanctify this unity, would touch,
    stroke, cling, fuse?

Conscience

In how many of the miserable little life dramas I play out in my mind am
      I unforgivable,
despicable, with everything, love, kin, companionship, negotiable, market-
      able, for sale,
and yet I do forgive myself, hardly marking it, although I still remember
      those fierce
if innocently violent fantasies of my eternal adolescence which could
      nearly knock me down
and send me howling through myself for caves of simple silence, blackness,
      oblivion.
The bubble hardens, the opacities perfected: no one in here anymore to
      bring accusation,
no sob of shame to catch us in its throat, no omniscient angel, either, poor
      angel, child,
tremulous, aghast, covering its eyes and ears, compulsively washing out
      its mouth with soap.

Noise: Sinalunga

The cry of a woman making love in a room giving onto our hotel court-
      yard sounds just like Jed,
who has bronchitis, if he were saying "Ow!" in his sleep, loudly, from his
      room across the hall,
and so I am awake through another dawn in another small town in the
      country near Siena,
waiting for my son to wake up, too, and cough, or after weeks of this,
      please, not cough.
Now church bells from a nearby village; now sparrows, swallows, voices
      from a kitchen door,
as brilliant in the brilliant air as Cortona's Fra Angelico's *Annunciation's*
      scroll of angel speech.
Now an underpowered motorscooter on a hill and from the jukebox in the
      broken-down café,
the first still blessedly indecipherable traces of the ubiquitous American
      I-Loved-You rock . . .

Anger

I killed the bee for no reason except that it was there and you were watch-
ing, disapproving,
which made what I would do much worse but I was angry with you any-
way and so I put my foot on it,
leaned on it, tested how much I'd need to make that resilient, resisting
cartridge give way
and *crack!* abruptly, shockingly it did give way and you turned sharply
and sharply now
I felt myself balanced in your eyes—why should I feel myself so balanced
always in your eyes;
isn't just this half the reason for my rage, these tendencies of yours, sus-
ceptibilities of mine?—
and "Why?" your eyes said, "Why?" and even as mine sent back my an-
swer, "None of your affair,"
I knew that I was being once again, twice now, weighed, and this time
anyway found wanting.

Even So

Though she's seventy-four, has three children, five grown grandchildren
(one already pregnant),
though she married and watched two men die, ran a good business—
camping goods, tents,
not established and left to her by either of the husbands: it was her idea
and her doing—
lived in three cities, and, since retiring, has spent a good part of the time
traveling:
Europe, Mexico, even China, at the same time as Arthur Miller (though
she didn't see him),
even so, when the nice young driver of their bus, starting out that day
from Amsterdam,
asks her if she'd like to sit beside him in the jump seat where the ill tour
guide should sit,
she's flattered and flustered and for a reason she's surprised about, feels
herself being proud.

Drought

A species of thistle no one had ever seen before appeared almost overnight
 in all the meadows,
coarse, gray-greenish clumps scattered anywhere the dying grass had
 opened up bare earth.
The farmers knew better or were too weary to try to fight the things, but
 their children,
walking out beside them through the sunset down the hillsides toward the
 still cool woods
along the narrowed brooks, would kick the plants or try to pry them out
 with pointed sticks:
the tenacious roots would hardly ever want to give, though, and it was too
 hot still to do much more
than crouch together where the thick, lethargic water filtered up and ran
 a few uncertain feet,
moistening the pebbles, forming puddles where the thriving insects could
 repose and reproduce.

End of Drought

It is the opposite or so of the friendly gossip from upstairs who stops by
 every other evening.
It's the time she comes in once too often, or it's more exactly in the middle
 of her tête-à-tête,
when she grows tedious beyond belief, and you realize that unless an eti-
 quette is violated
this will just go on forever, the way, forever, rain never comes, then comes,
 the luscious opposite,
the shock of early drops, the pavements and the rooftops drinking, then
 the scent, so heady with release
it's almost overwhelming, thick and vaginal, and then the earth, terrified
 that she'd bungled it,
that she'd dwelt too long upon the problems of the body and the mind,
 the ancient earth herself,
like someone finally touching pen to page, breathes her languid, aching
 suspiration of relief.

Easter

As though it were the very soul of rational human intercourse which had
　　been violated,
I can't believe you did that, the father chokes out to his little son, kneeling
　　beside him,
tugging at the waistband of the tiny blue jeans, peering in along the split
　　between the buttocks,
putting down his face at last to sniff, then saying it again, with quiet indig-
　　nation, outrage,
a power more moral than parental: at issue here are covenants, agree-
　　ments from the dawn of time.
The child, meanwhile, his eyes a little wider than they might be, is other-
　　wise unblinking;
all the time the father raves, he stares, scholarly, detached, at a package
　　in his hands:
a box of foil-wrapped chocolate eggs, because it's spring, because the god
　　has died, and risen.

Girl Meets Boy

She would speak of "our relationship" as though it were a thing apart from
　　either of us,
an entity with separate necessities, even its own criteria for appraisal,
　　judgment, mode of act,
to which both of us were to be ready to sacrifice our own more momentary
　　notions of identity.
It was as though there were a pre-existent formula or recipe, something
　　from a textbook,
which demanded not only the right ingredients—attentiveness, affection,
　　generosity, et cetera—
but also a constant and rigorous examination and analysis of the shifting
　　configurations
our emotions were assuming in their presumed movement toward some
　　ultimate consummation
in whose intensity the rest of this, not an end, would be redeemed, to
　　wither quietly away.

Bishop Tutu's Visit to the White House: 1984

I am afraid for you a little, for your sense of shame; I feel you are accus-
tomed to ordinary evil.
Your assumption will be that disagreeing with your methods, he will
nevertheless grasp the problems.
You will assume that he will be involved, as all humans must be, for what
else is it to be human,
in a notion of personal identity as a progress toward a more conscious, in-
clusive spiritual condition,
so that redemption, in whatever terms it might occur, categorically will
have been earned.
How will you bear that for him and those around him, righteousness and
self are *a priori* the same,
that to have stated one's good intentions excuses in advance from any
painful sense of sin?
I fear you will be wounded by his obtuseness, humiliated by his pride,
mortified by his absurd power.

Experience

After a string of failed romances and intensely remarked sexual adven-
tures she'd finally married.
The husband was a very formal man, handsome, elegant . . . perhaps to
my taste too much so;
I sensed too much commitment in him to a life entailing . . . handsomeness
and elegance, I suppose,
but he was generous with her and even their frequent arguments had a
manageable vehemence.
She smiled often in those days, but behind her face an edge of animation
seemed nailed shut.
You wouldn't really worry for her, by now you knew she'd be all right, but
there were moments
when for no reason you could put your finger on you'd feel something in
yourself too rigidly attentive:
it was as though some soft herd-alarm, a warning signal from the species,
had been permanently tripped.

Resentment

What is there which so approaches an art form in its stubborn patience, its devotion to technique,
to elegant refinement: that relentless searching for receptacles to capture content and expression?
The fiercest lust of self toward self: is there anything which keeps the soul so *occupied*?
My slights, affronts: how I shuffle and reshuffle them, file them, index, code, and collate.
Justification, accusation: I permutate, elaborate, combine, condense, re-focus, re-refine.
I mull, I ponder, convince, cajole; I prove, disprove, accomplish, reaccomplish, satisfy, solve.
Begin again: courageous, unflinching, resigned, my conscience swooning with projected ingenuities;
my mind's two mouths, their song, their kiss, this inaccomplishable, accomplished consummation!

Mornings: Catherine

Sometimes she'd begin to sing to herself before she was out of bed, before, I can remember thinking
as I listened from my table in the other room, she really could have even been all the way awake:
no sound of sheets pulled back, footsteps, just her voice, her song, so soft at first I wasn't sure,
rising from the silence but so close to being in it still that I couldn't hear the words,
only the threads of melody a car passing or a child crying in another house would brush away,
until it would insist again, or I'd think it would, with the volume of a breeze, the odor of a breeze . . .
Waiting to hear it again, to hear her again, I wouldn't move, I'd almost, yes, hold my breath:
her voice, her song, the meshings and unmeshings with the attending world, with my incredulity.

The Ladder

God was an accident of language, a quirk of the unconscious mind, but
    unhappily never of my mind.

God had risen from dream, was dream, was a dream I wanted, would do
    much to have, but never had had.

Therefore, or maybe therefore, God became functioned, with want, with
    lack, with need, denial.

Then therefore, maybe therefore, equations: God and death, God and
    war, God injustice, hatred, pain.

Then my only revelation, knowing that if God did speak what He'd say
    would be, *Your heart is dull.*

I let my sophistries and disputations fail: I knew that only in His own fire
    would God be consumed.

God, a sheet of paper scrawled with garbled cipher, flared, then cooled to
    cinder, then the cinder,

pounded by these hammerings, blended with the textures of my—could I
    still say "soul"?—my soul.

War

Jed is breathlessly, deliriously happy because he's just been deftly am-
    bushed and gunned down

by his friend Ha Woei as he came charging headlong around the corner
    of some bushes in the *bois.*

He slumps dramatically to the ground, disregarding the damp, black,
    gritty dirt he falls into,

and holds the posture of a dead man, forehead to the earth, arms and legs
    thrown full-length east and west,

until it's time for him to rise and Ha Woei to die, which Ha Woei does
    with vigor and abandon,

flinging himself down, the imaginary rifle catapulted from his hand like
    Capa's Spanish soldier's.

Dinnertime, bath time, bedtime, story time: *bam, bambambam, bam*—
    Akhilleus and Hektor.

Not until the cloak of night falls do they give themselves to the truces
    and forgivenesses of sleep.

Greed

A much-beaten-upon-looking, bedraggled blackbird, not a starling, with a
    mangled or tumorous claw,
an extra-evil air, comically malignant, like something from a folktale meant
    to frighten you,
gimps his way over the picnic table to a cube of moist white cheese into
    which he drives his beak.
Then a glister of licentious leering, a conspiratorial gleam, the cocked
    brow of common avarice:
he works his yellow scissors deeper in, daring doubt, a politician with his
    finger in the till,
a weapon maker's finger in the politician, the slobber and the licking and
    the champ and click.
It is a lovely day, it always is; the innocent daylight fades into its dying,
    it always does.
The bird looks up, death-face beside the curded white, its foot, its fist of
    dying, daintily raised.

The Past

The past is not dependent on us for existence, but exists in its own right.
—HENRY STEELE COMMAGER

All along certainly it's been there, waiting before us, waiting to receive us,
    not to waver,
flickering shakily across the mind-screen, always in another shadow, al-
    ways potentially illusion,
but out ahead, where it should be, redeemable, retrievable, accessible not
    by imagination's nets
but by the virtue of its being, simply being, waiting patiently for us like
    any other unattended,
any other hardly anticipated or not even anticipated—as much as any
    other fact rolling in . . .
All the project needs is patience, cunning, similar to that with which we
    outwit trembling death . . .
Not "history" but scent, sound, sight, the sensual fact, the beings and the
    doings, the heroes,
unmediated now, the holy and the horrid, to be worked across not like a
    wistful map, but land.

Ice

Whatever the argument the young sailor on the train is having and whom-
ever with, he's not winning.
In his silly white starched French recruit's suit with its outsized bib and
teeny ribboned cap,
he looks endearingly anachronistic, like a deckhand in *Potemkin* in the
calm before they rise,
but he's gesticulating, striking one hand into the other, his feet tapping
out separate rhythms,
and he's whispering, pleading, fervently, intensely, sometimes with a sweet,
almost goofy grin,
sometimes angrily, most often angrily, or desperately, trying to convince
himself of something,
or someone else of something, something or someone more important than
he'd ever dreamed he'd know,
so it's frightening to wonder what it is, who it is, to elicit winces like that,
like a lion's roar.

The Modern

Its skin tough and unpliable as scar, the pulp out of focus, weak, granular,
powdery, blank,
this tomato I'm eating—wolfing, stuffing down: I'm so hungry—is horrible
and delicious.
Don't tell me, I know all about it, this travesty-sham; I know it was plucked
green and unripe,
then was locked in a chamber and gassed so it wouldn't rot till I bought it
but I don't care:
I was so famished before, I was sucking sweat from my arm and now my
tomato is glowing inside me.
I muscle the juice through my teeth and the seeds to the roof of my mouth
and the hard,
scaly scab of where fruit met innocent stem and was torn free I hold on
my tongue and savor,
a coin, a dot, the end of a sentence, the end of the long improbable utter-
ance of the holy and human.

The Mistress

After the drink, after dinner, after the half-hour idiot kids' cartoon special
    on the TV,
after undressing his daughter, mauling at the miniature buttons on the
    back of her dress,
the games on the bed—"Look at my pee-pee," she says, pulling her thighs
    wide, "isn't it pretty?"—
after the bath, pajamas, the song and the kiss and the telling his wife it's
    her turn now,
out now, at last, out of the house to make the call (out to take a stroll, this
    evening's lie),
he finds the only public phone booth in the neighborhood's been savaged,
    receiver torn away,
wires thrust back up the coin slot to its innards, and he stands there, what
    else? what now?
and notices he's panting, he's panting like an animal, he's breathing like a
    bloody beast.

The Lover

When she stopped by, just passing, on her way back from picking up the
    kids at school,
taking them to dance, just happened by the business her husband owned
    and her lover worked in,
their glances, hers and the lover's, that is, not the husband's, seemed so
    decorous, so distant,
barely, just barely touching their fiery wings, their clanging she thought
    so well muffled,
that later, in the filthy women's bathroom, in the stall, she was horrified to
    hear two typists
coming from the office laughing, about them, all of them, their boss, her
    husband, "the blind pig,"
one said, and laughed, "and her, the horny bitch," the other said, and they
    both laughed again,
"and *him*, did you see *him*, that sanctimonious, lying bastard—I thought
    he was going to *blush*."

Religious Thought

for (. . .)

Beyond anything else, he dwells on what might inhabit his mind at the
    moment of his death,
that which he'll take across with him, which will sum his being up as he's
    projected into spirit.
Thus he dwells upon the substance of his consciousness, what its contents
    are at any moment:
good thoughts, hopefully, of friends, recent lovers, various genres of at-
    tempted bliss.
Primitive notions of divinity and holy presence interest him not at all;
    blessèd, cursèd: less.
For life: a public, fame, companionship, arousal; for death, an endless
    calm floating on abyss.
His secret is the terror that mind will do to him again what it did that un-
    forgivable once.
Sometimes, lest he forget, he lets it almost take him again: the vile
    thoughts, the chill, the dread.

Carpe Diem

A young tourist with a two-thousand-dollar Leica and a nice-looking girl
    waiting outside the gate
has slipped into the park next to St.-Germain-des-Prés to take a picture
    with his super-fisheye
of a little girl in smock and sandals trying to balance herself on the low
    wrought-iron fence
in front of Picasso's statue for Apollinaire, the row of disattached Gothic
    arches as background.
He needs an awfully long time to focus; before you know it, she's circled
    all the way around
to the sunny bench where her mother sits intently probing at her big toe
    with a safety pin
and where a grungy Danish hippie is sound asleep, his head propped side-
    ways on his old guitar.
Wait, now we're changing lenses; uh oh, girlfriend's impatient: Okay, she
    says, let's move it, maestro!

Twins

"There were two of them but nobody knew at first because only one hap-
     pened on the table,
the other was just suddenly there during the night: I felt a spasm I thought
     or dreamed
had something to do with whatever they'd done to me that afternoon and
     then there it was.
I woke up—I suppose I should have called the nurse but all I did was
     turn the light on.
He wasn't breathing, it didn't occur to me to wonder dead or not dead: I
     was very tired.
I covered us again and dozed on and off till morning; when the nurse did
     come, she was angry.
Funny: I used to think one of them was yours, the other . . . you know . . .
     That solved something for me.
That and dope, dear, darling dope: I stayed stoned an entire month, then
     I bought my diaphragm."

The Telephone

He must be her grandson: they're both very dark, she with high, broad
     cheekbones, white wiry hair,
he slightly fairer, finer featured, hair thick, rich, black, badly cropped,
     shining with oil.
I'm only watching from my car so I can't tell what language they're in,
     but it's not English.
They're standing by the phone booth arguing, the boy apparently doesn't
     want to make the call,
but the woman takes his arm—she's farm-wife muscular, he's very lean—
     and easily shoves him in.
Very rapidly, with an offhanded dexterity, he punches out a number, lis-
     tens for hardly a moment
and with an I-told-you-so exasperation holds out the receiver so that she
     can lean to it,
not quite touching, and listen, eyes focused to the middle distance, for at
     least a dozen rings.

Failure

Maybe it's not as bad as we like to think: no melodramatic rendings, sack-
 cloths, nothing so acute
as the fantasies of conscience chart in their uncontrollably self-punishing
 rigors and admonitions.
Less love, yes, but what was love: a febrile, restless, bothersome trembling
 to continue to possess
what one was only partly certain was worth wanting anyway, and if the
 reservoir of hope is depleted,
neither do distracting expectations interfere with these absorbing medita-
 tions on the frailties of chance.
A certain *resonance* might be all that lacks; the voice spinning out in dark-
 ness in an empty room.
The recompense is knowing that at last you've disconnected from the nar-
 ratives that conditioned you
to want to be what you were never going to be, while here you are still
 this far from "the end."

Crime

John the tailor had gone racing up the stairs in back of his store and be-
 cause he was so frightened
had jumped right out the window into the street where he broke his arm,
 though not badly.
A mounted policeman who'd been with his married girlfriend around the
 corner heard the shouts
and came cantering up just as the holdup man with a pistol in his hand
 was coming out:
the policeman pulled his gun, shot once, hit the robber in the chest, and
 it was over.
By the time I got there, everybody was waiting for the ambulance, John
 was still sobbing,
the crook was lying next to that amazing clot of blood, congealed to the
 consistency of cow plop,
and kids were darting from the crowd, scrambling for the change he'd let
 spill when he fell.

Fat

The young girl jogging in mittens and skimpy gym shorts through a freez-
    ing rainstorm up our block
would have a perfect centerfold body except for the bulbs of grand-
    motherly fat on her thighs.
Who was it again I loved once . . . no, not loved truly, liked, somewhat,
    and slept with, a lot,
who when she'd brood on the I thought quite adorable blubber she had
    there would beat it on the wall?
Really: she'd post herself naked half a stride back, crouch like a skier, and
    swing her hips, bang!
onto the plaster, bang! ten times, a hundred: bang! the wall shook, bang!
    her poor body quivered.
I'd lie there aghast, I knew that mad pounding had to mean more than
    itself, of course I thought me.
For once I was right; soon after, she left me, and guess what, for all that,
    I missed her.

Fame

I recognize the once-notorious radical theater director, now suffering gen-
    eral public neglect
but still teaching and writing and still certain enough of his fame so that
    when I introduce myself
he regards me with a polite, if somewhat elevated composure, acknowl-
    edging some friends in common,
my having heard him lecture once, even the fact that I actually once
    dashed off a play
inspired by some of his more literary speculations, but never does he ask
    who I might be,
what do, where live, et cetera, manifesting instead that maddeningly bland
    and incurious cosmopolitan
or at least New Yorkian self-centeredness, grounded in the most unshak-
    able and provincial syllogism:
I am known to you, you not to me, therefore you clearly must remain be-
    neath serious consideration.

USOCA

At the United States Out of Central America rally at a run-down community center in the Village

the audience is so sparse that the Andean musicians who've come to play for us are embarrassed

and except for the bass guitarist who has to give the introductions explaining their songs

they all focus resolutely on their instruments, their gazes never rising, even to one another.

Their music is vital, vigorous, sometimes almost abandoned, but informed always with nostalgia,

with exile's dark alarms and melancholy, exacerbated surely by how few and weak we are

but which we disregard, applauding when they're done so heartfeltly that they relent a bit,

releasing shy, exotic smiles for us to pass along between us like the precious doves of hope.

Eight Months

Jed is having his bath; he lies in a few inches of water in his plastic bathtub on the kitchen sink.

Catherine holds a bar of white soap in one hand, her other hand rubs it, then goes to Jed,

slipping over his gleaming skin, the bulges and crevasses, back to the soap, back to Jed.

She's humming, Jed is gazing raptly at her and every time her hand leaves for its journey,

he squirms with impatience, his own hands follow along as though to hurry her return to him.

When he realizes I'm in the room, he smiles brilliantly up at me, welcoming me into the ritual.

Catherine stops crooning, looks up too, smiles too, but her hand goes on, moving over Jed,

the soap, Jed, gently roiling the foamy surface: before I'm out the door, she's singing again.

Junior High School Concert: Salle Rossini

Each movement of the Mozart has a soloist and as each appears the con-
    ductor tunes her instrument,
while they, pubescent girls all, look fiercely unconcerned with being pos-
    sibly made fools of.
Their teacher is oblivious to that, though with his graying dentures he
    seems kind enough,
he just loves music more—you can tell he might love music more than
    Toscanini or than Bach.
It might be the saddest thing about the arts that they so seldom recom-
    pense passion and commitment
with genius or with anything at all beyond a ground-floor competence, but
    tant pis! for that,
the old man seems to say, *Tant pis!* too if the cellos thump, if the *lento* is
    a trifle tired,
if the girl slogging through as soon would let the whole thing drop: *Tant
    pis!* everything: *Bravo!*

The Prodigy

for Elizabeth Bishop

Though no shyer than the others—while her pitch is being checked she
    beams out at the audience,
one ear sticking through her fine, straight, dark hair, Nabokov would sure
    say "deliciously"—
she's younger, slimmer, flatter, still almost a child: her bow looks half a
    foot too big for her.
Not when she begins to play, though: when she begins to play, when she
    goes swooping, leaping,
lifting from the lumbering *tutti* like a fighter plane, that bow is fire, that
    bow is song,
that bow lifts all of us, father and old uncle, yawning younger brother and
    bored best friend,
and brings us all to song, to more than song, to breaths breathed for us,
    sharp, indrawn,
and then, as she bows it higher and higher, to old sorrows redeemed, a
    sweet sensation of joy.

Souls

Bound with baling wire to the tubular jerry-built bumper of a beat-up old
dump truck
are two of those gigantic teddy bears people win (usually shills) in cheap
amusement parks.
It's pouring: dressed in real children's clothes, they are, our mothers would
have said, drenched,
and they're also unrelentingly filthy, matted with the sticky, sickly, ghastly,
dark gray sheen
you see on bums ambulating between drinking streets and on mongrels
guarding junkyards.
Their stuffing hasn't been so crushed in them as to affect their jaunty, open-
armed availability,
but, regarded more closely, they seem to manifest a fanatical expression-
lessness, like soldiers,
who, wounded, captured, waiting to be shipped away or shot, must sub-
mit now to their photograph.

Regret

Rather die than live through dying with it: rather perish absolutely now
than perish partially
in its cold coils which would mean savaging the self from far within where
only love, self-love,
should be allowed to measure what one was and is and to roll the bales of
loss aside.
Or if it should survive to insinuate itself into that ceremony: not to have
to own to it,
not to any other, anyway, at least to keep the noble cloak of reticence
around one's self,
keep the self-contained and self-sustaining version of what was not en-
dured but was accomplished.
Never rue: that old longing rather that the past would be always the portal
of touching possibility:
to say I am the life and was the life, to dying say I am still the matrix and
again the fire.

Cowboys

The science-fiction movie on the telly in which the world, threatened by
   aliens with destruction,
is, as always, saved is really just a Western with rays and jets instead of
   pistols and horses.
The heroes crouch behind computers instead of rocks, but still mow down
   the endlessly expendable villains
who fire back but somehow always miss the stars, except one, the extra-
   lovable second lead,
nice guy, funny, a little too libidinal, who you know from minute one will
   teach us to die,
in his buddy's arms, stoical, never losing sight of our side's virtues: com-
   munity and self-denial.
On the other channel, Pompeii: Christians, pagans, same story, them and
   us, another holy mission,
the actors resonating with deep conviction, voices of manly sanctity, like
   Reagan on the news.

The Marriage

The way she tells it, they were in the Alps or somewhere, tall, snow-capped
   mountains anyway,
in their hotel, a really nice hotel, she says, they'd decided that for once
   they'd splurge.
They'd just arrived, they were looking from their terrace out across a lake
   or bay or something.
She was sitting there, just sitting there and thinking to herself how pleas-
   ant it all looked,
like a postcard, just the way for once it's supposed to look, clean and pure
   and cool,
when his hand came to her shoulder and he asked her something, "Don't
   you think it's lovely?"
then something else, his tone was horrid; there was something that he
   wanted her to say—
how was *she* to know what he wanted her to say?—and he *shook* her then,
   until she ached.

Fifteen

for Jessie

You give no hint how shy you really are, so thoroughly your warm and
welcoming temperament masks
those confounding and to me still painful storms of adolescent ill at ease,
confusion and disruption.
Our old father-daughter stroll down South Street these days is like a foray
into the territories—
the weighings and the longings, young men, men of age, the brazen or
sidelong subliminal proposings:
you're fair game now, but if you notice, you manage to keep it unimpeach-
ably to yourself,
your newly braceless smile good-humoredly desexualizing the leering and
licentious out-there.
Innocently you sheathe yourself in the most patently innocuous and un-
premeditated innocence;
even with me, though, your kiss goodbye is layered: cheek toward, body
swayed imperceptibly away.

Sixteen: Tuscany

Wherever Jessie and her friend Maura alight, clouds of young men sud-
denly appear like bees.
We're to meet in Florence at the Ponte Vecchio at nine o'clock: they're
twenty minutes early,
two vacationing Sicilian bees, hair agleam like fenders, are begging for a
kiss good night when we arrive.
At San Gimignano, on the steps that go down from the church into the
square—such clean breezes—
two Tuscan bees, lighter, handsome: great flurried conferences with refer-
ences to pocket dictionary
to try to find out where we're staying, how long staying, how get there . . .
impossible, poor bees.
A broad blond bee from Berkeley at the bank in Lucca; in Pisa, French
bees, German bees . . .
The air is filled with promises of pollen, the dancing air is filled with
honeyed wings and light.

Thinking Thought

"Oh, soul," I sometimes—often—still say when I'm trying to convince my
inner self of something.

"Oh, soul," I say still, "there's so much to be done, don't want to stop to
rest now, not already.

"Oh, soul," I say, "the implications of the task are clear, why procrastinate,
why whine?"

All the while I know my struggle has to do with mind being only some-
times subject to the will,

that other portion of itself which manages to stay so recalcitrantly, obsti-
nately impotent.

"Oh, soul, come into my field of want, my realm of act, be attentive to my
computations and predictions."

But as usual soul resists, as usual soul retires, as usual soul's old act of dis-
sipation and removal.

Oh, the furious illusive unities of want, the frail, false fusions and discur-
sive chains of hope.

Jews

She could tell immediately, she said, that he was Jewish, although he
didn't of course *look* it,

it was his . . . seriousness—and she wanted to take the opportunity because
she met so few these days

to ask him some questions about the vision a Jew would have of some of
the unfortunate attitudes

she felt were being promulgated—oh, Lord, again—in this terribly pro-
vincial, conservative country.

She'd been a leftist in the old days, when it was still worth being one, she'd
admired Jews then

and still did: they were so much more aware of subtleties, of implications
in the apparently innocuous.

Here, for instance, the old anti-Semitism, little explicit, little said in public,
but people like us,

sensitive to that sort of thing, surely *we* knew: couldn't he sense it just in
the *tone* of things?

Snow: I

All night, snow, then, near dawn, freezing rain, so that by morning the
    whole city glistens
in a glaze of high-pitched, meticulously polished brilliance, everything
    rounded off,
the cars submerged nearly to their windows in the unbroken drifts lining
    the narrow alleys,
the buildings rising from the trunklike integuments the wind has molded
    against them.
Underlit clouds, blurred, violet bars, the rearguard of the storm, still hang
    in the east,
immobile over the flat river basin of the Delaware; beyond them, nothing,
    the washed sky,
one vivid wisp of pale smoke rising waveringly but emphatically into the
    brilliant ether.
No one is out yet but Catherine, who closes the door behind her and starts
    up the street.

Snow: II

It's very cold, Catherine is bundled in a coat, a poncho on top of that, high
    boots, gloves,
a long scarf around her neck, and she's sauntering up the middle of the
    snowed-in street,
eating, of all things, an apple, the blazing redness of which shocks against
    the world of white.
No traffic yet, the *crisp crisp* of her footsteps keeps reaching me until she
    turns the corner.
I write it down years later, and the picture still holds perfectly, precise,
    unwanting,
and so too does the sense of being suddenly bereft as she passes abruptly
    from my sight,
the quick wash of desolation, the release again into the memory of affec-
    tion, and then affection,
as the first trucks blundered past, chains pounding, the first delighted chil-
    dren rushed out with sleds.

Gardens

The ever-consoling fantasy of my early adolescence was that one day time
    would stop for me:
everything in the world, for however long I wanted it to, would stay frozen
    in a single instant,
the clock on the classroom wall, the boring teacher, the other kids . . . all
    but someone else and me,
Arlene and me, Marie and me, Barbara of the budding breasts, Sheila of
    the braids and warming smile . . .
In the nurse's room there was a narrow cot, there we would repair, there
    we would reveal ourselves.
One finds of course to one's amazement and real chagrin that such things
    actually happen,
the precocious male, the soon to be knocked-up girl, but by now that's no
    longer what we care about:
what matters now are qualities of longing, this figment, fragment, its pre-
    cious, adorable irresolutions.

The Star

Though he's sitting at the restaurant bar next to the most startlingly glam-
    orous woman in the place,
who keeps leaning against him, alertly, conscientiously, even solemnly at-
    tending his every word,
the very famous ex-basketball player, when he isn't dealing directly with
    her or one of his friends,
seems enormously distracted—whenever he can retreat into himself he
    does, his eyes drift away,
he takes great care to listen to what's said but the listening never really
    overtakes the waiting,
for whatever is happening to be finished so that something new can hap-
    pen, something different, else:
even when strangers stop to offer homage, to pass a moment in his pres-
    ence, though he's gracious,
his attention never quite alights but stays tensed away, roving his dissatis-
    factions like a cat.

Kin

"You make me sick!" this, with rancor, vehemence, disgust—again, "You
   hear me? *Sick!*"
with rancor, vehemence, disgust again, with rage and bitterness, arrogance
   and fury—
from a little black girl, ten or so, one evening in a convenience market, to
   her sister,
two or three years younger, who's taking much too long picking out her
   candy from the rack.
What next? Nothing next. Next the wretched history of the world. The
   history of the heart.
The theory next that all we are are stories, handed down, that all we are
   are parts of speech.
All that limits and defines us: our ancient natures, love and death and
   terror and original sin.
And the weary breath, the weary going to and fro, the weary always know-
   ing what comes next.

Fire

The boss, the crane operator, one of the workers, a friend of somebody in
   the junkyard—
whoever it is who watches me when I pull up to see the fire in the cab of
   the huge derrick,
the flames in crisp, hungry, emphatic shapes scaling the suddenly fragile-
   ribbed steel tower,
considers it a matter of deep, real suspicion that a stranger should bother
   to want to see this:
slouched against a stack of rusty, dismembered fenders, he regards me
   with a coolness bordering threat,
a wariness touching frank hostility, while, from a low warehouse building
   across the street,
another person, with a bulky fire extinguisher, comes, like someone from
   the UN, running,
red-faced, panting, with a look of anxious desperation, as though all the
   fault were his.

Dignity

It only exists in us so that we may lose it but then not lose it, never at all
    costs lose it:
no matter what the gaffe or awful error that we've made, on the spot we
    reassume ourselves
rapidly enough to reconvince ourselves it never happened, never could
    have happened, until,
perhaps, much later, in another life, another universe, one lonely evening,
    gently reminiscing,
sweetly sorrowing for this, sweetly fondling that, something brings to mind
    another night,
that night, when you lost . . . what? your composure? yes, you'd thought
    then you'd lost composure,
yes, the muscles of your stomach knotted up against your ribs, your hands
    trembled, but now you know
you lost more than that, yes, much more than that, but that was then,
    surely not again, never *now*.

Fast Food

Musingly she mouths the end of her ballpoint pen as she stares down at
    the sheet of paper.
A job application: lines, boxes, blanks to fill, a set of instructions, that logo
    at the top.
Name and address, she's got that; phone number, age, high school, height
    and weight: that.
Then number problems, addition, subtraction, a long, long division . . .
    she hasn't got that.
It's blank next to that, the page is white next to that, her eyes touch down
    on the white near that.
Never so white was white as that white: oh, white, angel of white, never
    were you so pure,
never were you so seared by anyone's eyes and never so sadly bereft when
    eyes lifted away,
when eyes left you and moved, indifferent and cool, across you to the wait-
    ing door, oh, white, white.

The Orchid

with thanks to Curtis Ingham

"Tell me to touch your breast," I wanted to say: "Please, please, please
    touch my breast,"
I thought she wanted to say, but was too frightened, like me, too over-
    whelmed, too stricken,
like me, with the surges and furies of need; our lips, locked, ground to-
    gether again and again,
we were bruised and swollen, like lovers in stories, sweating like lovers in
    bed, but no bed.
Then I heard, I thought, "Touch me," and ecstatic, I touched, but she
    brushed me away like a fly . . .
No, still held me, only my hand fell like a fly, her thirsty lips drank from
    me what they needed.
My testicles trembled, the orchid I'd paid five dollars for, hooked to the
    wires of her bra,
browned, faded, crumpled between us, as the orchid of memory crumples,
    mummified like a fly.

The City in the Hills

Late afternoon and difficult to tell if those are mountains, soft with mist,
    off across the lake,
the day's last luminosity pale over them, or if a dense, low-lying cloudbank
    is holding there,
diffusing the dusk above the cottages scattered charmingly on the just-
    discernible far shore.
A tumultuous quiet chimney of shrilly shrieking starlings wheeling and
    turning over the wharves
abruptly unwinds a single undulating filament that shoots resolutely and
    unwaveringly across,
and now the old white steamer with its grainy voice of sentiment and
    resignation sets off too,
to fetch the happy-ending humans implied so richly by the tiled roofs
    against the pines behind
and by the autumn air, its biting balm sensualized now by the inhalations
    of the eager evening.

From the Next Book by (...)

... The part where he's telling himself at last the no longer deniable truth
 about himself.
He's remembering his sins, the grosser ones he sublimated for characters
 and conflicts,
and the hardly noticeable omissions, especially from his early time, which
 he realizes now
he tended, cultivated: seeds of something which would someday bear fruit,
 achieve their grandeur.
And the woman he had lived with, and was trapped by and suffered from
 (not with), that omission . . .
Something was the matter with her heart, the doctors said, she'd need an
 operation . . .
She comes awake, sobbing in the night, holding him (although he really
 can't be held by now),
telling him she doesn't want to die, and him (this is the confession) aston-
 ished she'd care.

Native Americans

I'm not sure whether it was Hiawatha or a real Indian who so impressed
 me during my latency.
My father would read me Longfellow; one of our teachers taught us actual
 reservation life,
to try to make us understand that our vision of exotics and minorities was
 so contaminated
that we not only had corrupted ideas of history but didn't know what went
 on under our noses.
Whatever the person I derived from all that, I was very moved by how
 seriously he comported himself:
whether I really wanted to be him, or like him, with that intimidating valor
 and self-possession,
aren't really questions at this late date, but maybe that elaborate identity,
 warrior, victim,
hunter, obstinate survivor, muddled, split, meant more to me than just
 another semblance to be shed.

Work

Although constructed of the most up-to-date, technically advanced ele-
ments of woven glass,
carrying messages by laser pulse, the cable the telephone men are thread-
ing down the manhole
has exactly the same thickness and tense flexibility and has to be handled
with the same delicacy
as the penis of the huge palamino stallion I saw breeding at the riding
school when I was twelve
who couldn't get it in so that Charlie Young the little stablehand had to
help him with it.
How more than horrified I was that Charlie would touch the raw, unpeeled,
violet-purple thing,
thinking nothing of it, slipping between the flaring, snorting stud and the
gleaming mare,
lascivious and elegant, who, sidling under now, next year would throw a
mediocre foal, soon sold.

Gratitude

for Steve Berg

I'm scribbling suggestions on a copy of the next-to-final draft of my friend's
book of poems.
When I stop to rest, rub my eyes, and look up out the window, the phone
company, at it again,
has a sort of miniature collapsible crane outside, one member, dangling
cables from its jaws,
looming weirdly in a long, smooth, effortless arc across my line of sight,
white, clean, sleek,
enameled steel, impeccable, like something from those science-fiction flicks
my kids are so insane for.
For a moment I let myself envy the people who make those films: all that
money, all that audience . . .
The poem I'm reading now is "Gratitude": "Sunday. Nothing to do. I park.
Stumps. Weeds . . ."
And there's nothing much to do here either: all the whole poem needed
was to cut a "the."

Will

The boy had badly malformed legs, and there was a long, fresh surgical
    scar behind one knee.
The father, frankly wealthy, quite young, tanned, very boardroom, very
    well-made, self-made,
had just taken the boy's thin arm the way you would take the arm of an
    attractive woman,
with firmness, a flourish of affection; he was smiling directly down into the
    boy's face
but it was evident that this much companionability between them wasn't
    usual, that the father,
whatever else his relation to the boy consisted of, didn't know that if you
    held him that way
you would overbalance him, which, when the boy's crutches splayed and
    he went down, crying "*Papa!*"
must have been what informed his voice with such shrill petulance, such
    anguished accusation.

Pregnant

Tugging with cocked thumbs at the straps of her old overalls the way hick
    movie-farmers used to,
"This is the only thing I can wear," she declares, the halter hard against
    her heavy breasts,
then her hands encircle the impressive eight months' globe slung in its sack
    of comfortable denim.
Not eighteen yet, she isn't so much radiant, as brides are (she's not mar-
    ried), as radiantly complacent:
her two friends seem moved by the charming self-attention she graciously
    allows them to share.
They watch closely as with affectionate familiarity she pushes on the fore-
    part of the bulge,
as though she already felt the brow and headshape there and was com-
    municating arcane greetings,
which she then subtleizes into that consoling feathery, obsessive gesture,
    effleurage.

Peace

We fight for hours, through dinner, through the endless evening, who even
    knows now what about,
what could be so dire to have to suffer so for, stuck in one another's craws
    like fishbones,
the cadavers of our argument dissected, flayed, but we go on with it, to bed,
    and through the night,
feigning sleep, dreaming sleep, hardly sleeping, so precisely never touch-
    ing, back to back,
the blanket bridged across us for the wintry air to tunnel down, to keep us
    lifting, turning,
through the angry dark that holds us in its cup of pain, the aching dark,
    the weary dark,
then, toward dawn, I can't help it, though justice won't I know be served,
    I pull her to me,
and with such accurate, graceful deftness she rolls to me that we arrive em-
    bracing our entire lengths.

Some of Us

How nearly unfeasible they make it for the rest of us, those who, with ex-
    actly our credentials,
attain, if that's how it happens, the world of the publicly glamorous, the
    very chic, the "in."
It isn't so much being omitted, left home from the party, as knowing that
    we'll never get there,
never participate in those heady proximities our insatiable narrations ever
    tremble toward.
What would be there, we ask ourselves. Better bosoms? Better living rooms?
    Contemptibles.
Still, without it, the uneasy sense of incompletion, not really to have lived
    all that was to live,
especially knowing at this age how easy it would be now to evade en-
    croachments of the essentials,
those once impressionable, now solitude-inured, scar-tissue tough tabulas
    of receptive ego.

Two: Resurrections

Jed kills Catherine with a pistol he's put together himself out of some plastic play blocks.

Bang! you're dead. Catherine falls down on the floor: Look, you've killed me now, she says.

Jed is neither amused nor upset, but there is something in all this he takes very seriously.

I want to kill you again, he says. Before you can, Catherine says, you'll have to fix me.

I'll fix you, Jed says, and runs into the bathroom, coming back with Catherine's comb and brush.

He kneels beside her and with great solemnity places the brush in the center of her chest.

Then, still silent, still very serious, he slowly runs the comb over her left breast, right breast,

then down her belly, once across the breadth of her hips, then deep into the valley of her crotch.

Men

As the garbage truck is backing up, one of the garbagemen is absorbed watching a pretty girl pass

and a sleeve of protruding steel catches him hard enough on the bicep to almost knock him down.

He clutches at his arm, limping heavily across the sidewalk, obviously in quite serious discomfort,

but the guy who works with him and who's seen the whole thing absolutely refuses to acknowledge

that his partner might be hurt, instead he bursts out laughing and starts making fun of the guy,

imitating the way he's holding himself, saying, "Booby-baby want a kiss? What's mattah, baby?"

Now the one who's hurt, grimacing, says, "Christ," shaking his head, vigorously rotating his arm.

Then, "You prick," he growls, and with a clunky leap and a great boom kicks the side of the truck.

Shame

A girl who, in 1971, when I was living by myself, painfully lonely, bereft, depressed,

offhandedly mentioned to me in a conversation with some friends that although at first she'd found me—

I can't remember the term, some dated colloquialism signifying odd, unacceptable, out-of-things—

she'd decided that I was after all all right . . . twelve years later she comes back to me from nowhere

and I realize that it wasn't my then irrepressible, unselective, incessant sexual want she meant,

which, when we'd been introduced, I'd naturally aimed at her and which she'd easily deflected,

but that she'd thought I really was, in myself, the way I looked and spoke and acted,

what she was saying, creepy, weird, whatever, and I am taken with a terrible humiliation.

On the Other Hand

On the other hand, in Philadelphia, long ago, at a party on Camac Street on a Sunday afternoon,

a springtime or an early autumn Sunday afternoon, I know, though the occasion's lost

and whose house it was is even lost, near the party's end, a girl, a woman, someone else's wife,

a beauty, too, a little older than I was, an "older woman," elegant and admirable and sober, too,

or nearly so, as I was coming down the stairs, put her hand on my hand on the landing,

caught me there and held me for a moment, with her hand, just her gentle hand, and with her look,

with how she looked at me, with some experience I didn't have, some delight I didn't understand,

and pulled me to her, hard, and kissed me, hard, to let me taste what subtle lusts awaited me.

The Fountain

Two maintenance men need half the morning probing just to find the an-
  cient cut-off valve
which is locked tight with rust so that they have to wrestle it with pene-
  trating oil and wrenches
until the flow begins to falter, then arrests, the level in the basin hesitantly
  lowering.
Now they shovel at the copper drains, mossed and caked with leaves and
  scraps of sandwich paper;
now a fishy fragrance fills the atmosphere although there weren't and never
  have been any fish,
and all the gods and goddesses, the Neptunes and the dolphins and Dianas,
  shed their sheen,
their streaked bronze re-emerging, dimmer now, paler, to its other element,
  while underneath,
a million filters from a million cigarettes tremble in the final suction, worm-
  ing at the slits.

The Latin Quarter

All the Greek restaurants in the old student neighborhood have pigs roast-
  ing in their windows.
From morning until dinnertime the plump sucklings deliciously darken,
  rotating dutifully
on the blackened spits which enter by the anus and exit from angry wounds
  between the eyes.
One's front legs have been neatly trussed beneath it, like a hunting horse
  from *Horn and Hound.*
Another's have been wittily arranged to cover its squinting eyes, like some-
  one being "it."
In one place, no pig, just a singer, on a platform on a stool: a young man
  with a *balalaika.*
On the floor in front of him, a television screen in grainy blues shows him
  again, but from behind,
so that, standing listening to his voice come through the squeaky speaker,
  we can be there, too.

Rungs

When we finally tracked him down, the old man (not really all that very
   old, we thought)
who'd made the comfortable, graceful, elegantly mortised chairs for all the
   farmers' kitchens
told us, never even opening the heavy iron gate into his yard, that he was
   through, retired,
done with it, and no, he didn't know anybody else who made them now,
   no one, he was the last.
He seemed to say it all with satisfaction, or at least was anyway unmoved
   by what it may have meant,
leaving us to back away, apologize, get into our car to make an awkward
   U-turn in his unpaved lane,
suffering meanwhile pangs of conscience and regret for honest good things
   gone for good,
all the innocence the world was losing, all the chances we'd once had, and
   lost, for beauty.

Normality

"Sometimes I feel as though all I really want is to take his little whizzer in
   my mouth . . .
Didn't you ever feel anything like that? I mean, I'll be changing him, and
   he's smiling,
kicking his legs like crazy, and I can tell he's really excited and I know *I'm*
   excited
and I think how clean and pure and soft he is down there, and that won-
   derful *smell*, you know,
at first you think it's the powder you put on them but then you realize it's
   them, *him*,
it's his goddamned intrinsic odor, I could eat it up, and what would be so
   wrong with it?
I'm not trying to shock you; I mean, maybe if you let yourself, you'd feel
   things like that . . .
Maybe it's you who's fucked up and repressed; I'll bet what I feel for my
   baby's *normal*."

The Storm

A dense, low, irregular overcast is flowing rapidly in over the city from the
    middle South.
Above it, the sky holds blue, with scattered, intricate conglomerations of
    higher clouds
sidling in a much more even, stately procession across the dazzling, unsul-
    lied azure.
Now the lower level momentarily thins, fragments, and the early sun, still
    sharply angled,
breaks through into a finer veil and simmers, edges sharp, its ardent disk
    gently mottled.
Down across the roof lines, the decorative dome of Les Invalides looms, in-
    truding on all this,
and suddenly a swallow banks around its gilded slopes, heading out but
    veering quickly back
as though the firmament, figured by so many volumes now, were too intim-
    idating to row out in alone.

Blame

Where no question possibly remains—someone crying, someone dead—
    blame asks: whose fault?
It is the counterpart, the day-to-day, the real life, of those higher faculties
    we posit,
logic, reason, the inductions and deductions we yearningly trace the lines
    of with our finger.
It also has to do with nothing but itself, a tendency, a habit, like smoking
    or depression:
the unaccountable life quirks forecast in neither the soured milk nor the
    parents' roaring bed.
Relationship's theodicy: as the ever-generous deity leaves the difficult door
    of faith ajar
in a gesture of just-fathomable irony, so our beloved other, in the pain of
    partial mutuality,
moves us with its querulous "Look what you made me do!" toward the first
    clear glimpses of terrible self.

Medusa

Once, in Rotterdam, a whore once, in a bar, a sailors' bar, a hooker bar,
    opened up her legs—
her legs, my god, were logs—lifted up her skirt, and rubbed herself, with
    both hands rubbed herself,
there, right there, as though what was there was something else, as though
    the something else
was something she just happened to have under there, something that she
    wanted me to see.
All I was was twenty, I was looking for a girl, the girl, the way we always,
    all of us,
looked for the girl, and the woman leaned back there and with both hands
    she mauled it,
talked to it, asked it if it wanted me, laughed and asked me if I wanted it,
    while my virginity,
that dread I'd fought so hard to lose, stone by stone was rising back inside
    me like a wall.

Rush Hour

Someone has folded a coat under the boy's head, someone else, an Arab
    businessman in not very good French,
is explaining to the girl, who seems to have discovered, like this, in the
    crowded Métro,
her lover is epileptic, that something must be done to keep the boy from
    swallowing his tongue:
he works a billfold between the rigidly clenched teeth as the kneeling girl
    silently looks on,
her expression of just-contained terror transfiguring her, generalizing her
    almost to the mythic,
the very image of our wonder at what can befall the most ordinary after-
    noon of early love.
The spasms quiet, the boy, his left ear scarlet from rubbing the wool, comes
    to, looks up at the girl,
and she, as the rest of us begin to move away, hesitates, then lays her
    cheek lightly on his brow.

Philadelphia: 1978

I'm on my way to the doctor to get the result of chest X-rays because I
    coughed blood
a few weeks ago while we were still in California; I am more or less a
    wreck of anxiety
and just as I turn the corner from Spruce Street onto Sixteenth where my
    doctor's is,
a raggedy-looking guy coming toward me on the sidewalk yells to me from
    fifty feet away:
"I know that walk! I sure know *that* walk!" smiling broadly, with genuine
    good feeling.
Although I don't recognize him—he looks druggy, wasted—I smile back,
    then, as we come closer,
he suddenly seems dubious, asking, "Don't I know you?" "Maybe not."
    "Weren't you in 'Nam?"
and before I can answer, "Shit!" he spits out, "shit!" furious with me: "You
    fucking *shit!*"

Midas

It wasn't any mewling squeamishness about how "hard" he'd become: if
    his responsibilities as chief
sometimes spilled over in impatience, with subordinates, even at home,
    well, that came with the territory.
And it wasn't either any unaccounted-for sentimentality, no degrading
    longings for the lost good days
when never enough had somehow been just enough, before more than he'd
    ever need became insufficient.
No, his preoccupation had to do with his desire: not with anything he
    wanted and didn't have—
what after all was left to have?—but with something askew in the very
    quality of desire itself.
It was as though he had to will himself to want, had to drag himself awake
    even to pay attention,
and then, when he'd ungaraged his lust, he'd half forget it, the ache would
    fade before it flowered.

The Park

In that oblivious, concentrated, fiercely fetal decontraction peculiar to the
    lost,
a grimy derelict is flat out on a green bench by the sandbox, gazing blankly
    at the children.
"Do you want to play with me?" a small boy asks another, his fine head
    tilted deferentially,
but the other has a lovely fire truck so he doesn't have to answer and em-
    phatically he doesn't,
he just grinds his toy, its wheels immobilized with grit, along the low stone
    wall.
The first child sinks forlornly down and lays his palms against the earth
    like Buddha.
The ankles of the derelict are scabbed and swollen, torn with aching vari-
    cose and cankers.
Who will come to us now? Who will solace us? Who will take us in their
    healing hands?

Travelers

He drives, she mostly sleeps; when she's awake, they quarrel, and now,
    in a violet dusk,
a rangy, raw-boned, efficient-looking mongrel loping toward them down
    the other shoulder
for no apparent reason swerves out on the roadbed just as a battered taxi
    is going by.
Horrible how it goes under, how it's jammed into the asphalt, compressed,
    abraded, crumpled,
then is ejected out behind, still, a miracle, alive, but spinning wildly on it-
    self, tearing,
frenzied, at its broken spine, the mindless taxi never slowing, never notic-
    ing or caring,
they slowing, only for a moment, though, as, "Go on," she says, "go on, go
    on," face averted,
she can't look, while he, guilty as usual, fearful, fascinated and uncouth,
    can't not.

Second Persons: Café de L'Abbaye

Without quite knowing it, you sit looking for your past or future in the
    couples strolling by,
the solitaries stalking by, saddened that you never seem to find what you've
    been looking for
although you've no idea or at least you tell yourself you don't what you
    might be looking for,
you only have the vaguest, vagrant sense that it would be someone you
    knew once, lover, friend,
and lost, let drift away, not out of your life, for they were meant to drift
    away that way,
but from some portion of your meaning to yourself, or from the place such
    meaning should reside:
the other would recuperate essences, would be the link from where you
    were to where you would be,
if consciousness were able, finally, to hold all of this together, even not
    quite ever knowing why.

The Lens

Snapshots of her grandchildren and great-grandchildren are scattered on
    the old woman's lap.
How are you, Ma? her son asks, then, before she answers, to the nurse:
    How's she doing?
The old woman, smiling, tilts her head back, centering her son in the thick,
    unfamiliar lenses.
Her head moves left, then right, farther back now, forward, then finally
    she has and holds him.
She is beaming now, an impression of almost too-rapt attentiveness, ad-
    miration, even adoration.
Do you want to eat, Ma? the son asks; the woman starts to nod and in
    doing so loses him again
and has to track him again, that same, slow, methodically circular, back-
    and-forth targeting in.
You want to go downstairs for lunch? the son asks, a bit impatient: Ma,
    you want to get a bite?

The Body

Jed says: How come I'm afraid to climb on the jungle game when even the
    littler kids aren't?

I say: But you did go up on it, I saw you before, you were going across the
    vine bridge.

Jed says: Yeah, I went up there, but I was afraid of the hard part, where
    you swing down.

I say: Well, people do things at different rates, there are things you can do
    that they can't.

Jed says: Am I a coward? Why couldn't I just swing right down there; I'm
    like the cowardly lion.

I say: When I was a kid I was just like you, I was always timid, I thought
    I was weak.

I say: I started doing sports late, like you, but look, now you're swimming
    and everything.

Jed says: I'm tired of swimming. What time is it? Can I get a crêpe? I don't
    think I'm weak.

Racists

Vas en Afrique! Back to Africa! the butcher we used to patronize in the
    rue Cadet market,

beside himself, shrieked at a black man in an argument the rest of the im-
    port of which I missed

but that made me anyway for three years walk an extra street to a shop of
    definitely lower quality

until I convinced myself that probably I'd misunderstood that other thing
    and could come back.

Today another black man stopped, asking something that again I didn't
    catch, and the butcher,

who at the moment was unloading his rotisserie, slipping the chickens off
    their heavy spit,

as he answered—how get this right?—casually but accurately *brandished*
    the still-hot metal,

so the other, whatever he was there for, had subtly to lean away a little, so
    as not to flinch.

The Dream

How well I have repressed the dream of death I had after the war when I
was nine in Newark.

It would be nineteen-forty-six; my older best friend tells me what the atom
bomb will do,

consume me from within, with fire, and that night, as I sat, bolt awake, in
agony, it did:

I felt my stomach flare and flame, the edges of my heart curl up and char
like burning paper.

All there was was waiting for the end, all there was was sadness, for in that
awful dark,

that roar that never ebbed, that frenzied inward fire, I knew that everyone
I loved was dead,

I knew that consciousness itself was dead, the universe shucked clean of
mind as I was of my innards.

All the earth around me heaved and pulsed and sobbed; the orient and
immortal air was ash.

Dawn

The first morning of mist after days of draining, unwavering heat along
the shore: a *breath*:

a plume of sea fog actually visible, coherent, intact, with all of the quieter
mysteries

of the sea implicit in its inconspicuous, unremarkable gathering in the
weary branches

of the drought-battered spruce on its lonely knoll; it thins now, sidles
through the browning needles,

is penetrated sharply by a sparrow swaying precipitously on a drop-glitter-
ing twiglet,

then another bird, unseen, is there, a singer, chattering, and another, long
purls of warble,

which also from out of sight insinuate themselves into that dim, fragile,
miniature cloud,

already now, almost with reluctance, beginning its dissipation in the over-
powering sunlight.

II

Reading: Winter

He's not sure how to get the jack on—he must have recently bought the
    car, although it's an ancient,
impossibly decrepit, barely holding-together Chevy: he has to figure out
    how each part works,
the base plate, the pillar, the thing that hooks to the bumper, even the four-
    armed wrench,
before he can get it all together, knock the hubcap off and wrestle free the
    partly rusted nuts.
This all happens on a bed of sheet ice: it's five below, the coldest January
    in a century.
Cars slip and skid a yard away from him, the flimsy jack is desperately,
    precariously balanced,
and meanwhile, when he goes into the trunk to get the spare, a page of
    old newspaper catches his attention
and he pauses, rubbing his hands together, shoulders hunched, for a full
    half minute, reading.

Reading: The Subway

First he finishes *The Chief*, "New York's Civil Employee's Weekly," then
    folds it carefully
and slips it into his much-wrinkled *Duane Reade* shopping bag ("The
    Chain of Experience"),
from which he retrieves a thick, green, double-cellophane-bound volume,
    Successful Investing,
balancing it on the waistband of his slick designer jeans: *Lewis*, they say,
    instead of *Levi's*.
The train is going very fast, the car sways frighteningly, almost lifting us
    from our seats,
but he stands firmly planted, with an imperturbably athletic dexterity, not
    even holding on,
only glancing up from time to time to gaze with an apparently real interest
    at an advertisement—
Un buen baño con jabón Ivory—as though to decathect a moment, letting
    go, the better to absorb.

Reading: The Bus

As she reads, she rolls something around in her mouth, hard candy it must
    be, from how long it lasts.
She's short, roundish, gray-haired, pleasantly pugnacious-looking, like
    Grace Paley, and her book,
Paint Good and Fast, must be fascinating: she hasn't lifted her eyes since
    Thirty-fourth Street,
even when the corner of a page sticks so that she has to pause a bit to lick
    her index finger . . .
No, now she does, she must have felt me thinking about her: she blinks,
    squints out the window,
violently arches her eyebrows as though what she'd just read had really to
    be nailed down,
and, stretching, she unzips a pocket of her blue backpack, rummages
    through it, and comes out with,
yes, hard candy, red and white, a little sackful, one of which she offers
    with a smile to me.

Reading: The Gym

The bench he's lying on isn't nearly wide enough for the hefty bulk of his
    torso and shoulders.
Shielding his eyes with his sheaf of scrawled-on yellow paper from the
    bare bulb over his head,
legs lifted in a dainty V, he looks about to tip, but catches himself with un-
    conscious shrugs.
Suddenly he rises—he's still streaming from his session on the Nautilus
    and heavy bag—
goes into the shower, comes back, dries off with a gray, too-small towel
    and sits to read again,
applying as he does an oily, evil-looking lotion from a dark brown bottle
    onto his legs and belly.
Next to his open locker, a ragged equipment bag, on top a paperback: *The
    Ethical System of Hume*.
The smell of wintergreen and steam-room steam; from the swimming pool
    echoes of children screaming.

Reading: The Cop

Usually a large-caliber, dull-black, stockless machine gun hangs from a
    sling at his hip
where a heavily laden cartridge belt in the same blue as his special-forces
    uniform cinches his waist,
and usually he stands directly in the doorway, so that people have to edge
    their way around him—
there was some sort of bombing in the building, and presumably this is
    part of his function.
He often seems ill at ease and seems to want to have but doesn't quite be-
    cause he's so young
that menacingly vacant expression policemen assume when they're unsure
    of themselves or lonely,
but still, today, when I noticed him back in the hallway reading what
    looked like a political pamphlet,
I was curious and thought I'd just stop, go back, peek in, but then I
    thought, no, not.

Reading: Early Sorrow

The father has given his year-old son *Le Monde* to play with in his stroller
    and the baby does
just what you'd expect: grabs it, holds it out in front of him, stares impor-
    tantly at it,
makes emphatic and dramatic sounds of declamation, great pronounce-
    ments of analytic probity,
then tears it, pulls a page in half, pulls the half in quarters, shoves a hearty
    shred in his mouth—
a delicious editorial on unemployment and recession, a tasty *jeu de mots*
    on government ineptitude.
He startles in amazement when the father takes the paper back from him:
    What in heaven's name?
Indignation, impotence, frustration, outrage, petulance, rebellion, realism,
    resignation.
Slumping back, disgusted . . . *Hypocrite lecteur, semblable* . . . Just wait,
    he's muttering, just wait . . .

Suicide: Elena

She was fourteen and a half; she'd hanged herself: how had she ever
    found the resource for it,
the sheer *strength*, as frail as she was, skinny even for her age, breastless
    and hipless,
with a voice so subdued and without resonance she seemed to play it to
    herself, like a clavichord?
My co-therapist had made a "megaphone" for her by tearing out the bot-
    tom of a paper coffee cup.
She agreed to try it, then seemed relieved to have it, becoming more volu-
    ble and animated.
She only visited our group once, though, with a boy I didn't see again un-
    til the day it happened.
"Do you know about Elena?" I asked him; I said the name the Spanish
    way, "El-*lay*-nah"—
I knew a Mexican Elena then, from Monterey—"El-*leh*-nah," the boy said,
    "not El-*lay*-nah. Yeah."

Suicide: Ludie

The whole time I've been walking down the block the public phone at the
    corner's been ringing
so when I get there just to try to help somebody out I stop and pick it up
    and say "Hello."
A woman's voice: "Is Ludie there?" "You have a wrong number," I answer,
    "I'm in a phone booth."
"I know you are," the voice says, "but isn't Ludie anywhere around there?"
    "No, no one is."
"You *sure*? Look again. She just called me, Ludie, and she says she's going
    to commit *su*-icide."
"She really isn't here, I'd have seen her down the street: there isn't any-
    body around here."
"Well, what am I supposed to do? What are you supposed to do when
    somebody's gonna kill herself?"
"The police. Where does Ludie live?" "That's the whole thing, she don't
    live where she lives."

Suicide: Anne

for Anne Sexton

Perhaps it isn't as we like to think, the last resort, the end of something,
     thwarted choice or attempt,
but rather the ever-recurring beginning, the faithful first to mind, the very
     image of endeavor,
so that even the most patently meaningless difficulties, a badly started
     nail, a lost check,
not to speak of the great and irresolvable emotional issues, would bring
     instantly to mind
that unfailingly reliable image of a gesture to be carried out for once with
     confidence and grace.
It would feel less like desperation, being driven down, ground down, and
     much more a reflex, almost whim,
as though the pestering forces of inertia that for so long had held you back
     had ebbed at last,
and you could slip through now, not to peace particularly, not even to es-
     cape, but to completion.

Love: Youth

Except for the undeniable flash of envy I feel, the reflexive competitive-
ness, he's inconsequential:
all I even see of him is the nape of his neck with his girlfriend's fingers
locked in his hair.
She, though, looks disturbingly like a girl I wanted and pestered and who
I thought broke my heart
when I was at that age of being all absorbed in just the unattainabilities
she represented.
With what unashamed ardor this one is kissing, head working, that hand
tugging him ever tighter,
and when at last they come apart, with what *gratitude* she peers at him,
staring into his eyes
with what looks like nothing but relief, as though she'd waited her whole
life for this, died for this,
time has taken so long for this, I thought you'd never get here, I thought
I'd wither first and fade.

Love: Beginnings

They're at that stage where so much desire streams between them, so much
frank need and want,
so much absorption in the other and the self and the self-admiring entity
and unity they make—
her mouth so full, breast so lifted, head thrown back *so* far in her laughter
at his laughter,
he so solid, planted, oaky, firm, so resonantly factual in the headiness of
being craved so,
she almost wreathed upon him as they intertwine again, touch again,
cheek, lip, shoulder, brow,
every glance moving toward the sexual, every glance away soaring back in
flame into the sexual—
that just to watch them is to feel again that hitching in the groin, that fill-
ing of the heart,
the old, sore heart, the battered, foundered, faithful heart, snorting again,
stamping in its stall.

Love: Habit

He has his lips pressed solidly against her cheek, his eyes are wide open,
     though, and she, too,
gazes into the distance, or at least is nowhere in the fragile composition
     they otherwise create.
He breaks off now, sulkily slouches back; his hand, still lifted to her face,
     idly cups her chin,
his fingers casually drumming rhythms on her lips, a gesture she finds not
     at all remarkable—
she still gazes away, looking for whatever she's been looking for, her in-
     attention like a wall.
Now he kisses her *again*, and they both, like athletes, hold that way again,
     perversely persevering . . .
Oh, Paolo, oh, Francesca: is this all it comes to, the perturbations and the
     clamor, the broken breath,
the careenings on the wheel: just this: the sorrowing flame of conscious-
     ness so miserably dimmed?

Love: Loss

He's the half-respectable wino who keeps to himself, camping with his
     bags on the steps of the *Bourse*.
She's the neighborhood schizo, our nomad, our pretty post-teen princess
     gone to the grim gutter:
her appalling matted hair, vile hanging rags, the engrossing shadow plays
     she acts out to herself.
Tonight, though, something takes her, she stops, waits, and smiling cun-
     ningly asks him for a smoke.
They both seem astonished, both their solitudes emerge, stiff-legged, blink-
     ing, from their lairs.
The air is charged with timid probings, promises, wants and lost wants,
     but suddenly she turns,
she can't do it, she goes, and he, with a stagy, blasé world-weariness leans
     back and watches,
like Orpheus watches as she raptly picks her way back to the silver path,
     back to the boiling whispers.

Love: Sight

When she's not looking in his eyes, she looks down at his lips, his chin, col-
lar, tie, back again.
When he's not looking in her eyes—her cheek, parted mouth, neck, breasts,
thighs, back again.
Sometimes their four hands will lock and in a smooth contortion end up at
her waist, then his waist,
then up between them, weaving, writhing, with so much animation that
their glances catch there.
The first time he looks away, she still smiles at him, smugly, with a lus-
ciousness almost obscene,
then her gaze goes trailing after, as if afraid to be abandoned, as if desir-
ing even what he sees.
The second time, it might be with some small suspicion that her eyes go
quickly chasing his;
the third, they're hardening, triangulating, calculating, like a combat ser-
geant's on the line.

Love: Petulance

She keeps taking poses as they eat so that her cool glance goes off at per-
pendiculars to him.
She seems to think she's hiding what she feels, that she looks merely in-
terested, sophisticated.
Sometimes she leans her head on her hand, sometimes with a single finger
covers her lower lip.
He, too, will prop his temple on his fist, as though to make her believe
he's lost in thought.
Otherwise he simply chews, although the muscles of his jaws rise violently
in iron ridges.
Their gazes, when they have to go that way, pass blankly over one an-
other like offshore lights.
So young they are for this, to have arrived at this, both are suffering so
and neither understands,
although to understand wouldn't mean to find relief or overcome, that
this, too, is part of it.

Love: Intimacy

They were so exceptionally well got-up for an ordinary Sunday afternoon
     stop-in at Deux Magots,
she in very chic deep black, he in a business suit, and they were so evi-
     dently just out of bed
but with very little to say to one another, much gazing off, elaborate light-
     ings of her cigarettes,
she more proper than was to be believed, sipping with a flourished pinky
     at her Pimm's Cup,
that it occurred to me I was finally seeing one of those intriguing *Herald
     Tribune* classifieds—
a woman's name, a number—for "escorts" or "companions," but then I
     had to change my mind:
she'd leaned toward him, deftly lifted a line of his thinning hair, and idly,
     with a mild pat,
had laid it back—not commiserating, really, just keeping record of the
     progress of the loss.

Love: Shyness

By tucking her chin in toward her chest, she can look up darkly through
     her lashes at him,
that look of almost anguished vulnerability and sensitivity, a soft, near-cry
     of help,
the implication of a deeply privileged and sole accessibility . . . yours alone,
     yours, yours alone,
but he's so flagrantly uncertain of himself, so clearly frightened, that he
     edges into comedy:
though everybody at the party is aware she's seducing him, he doesn't
     seem to understand;
he diddles with his silly mustache, grins and gawks, gabbles away around
     her about this and that.
Now she's losing interest, you can see it; she starts to glance away, can't
     he see it? Fool!
Touch her! Reach across, just caress her with a finger on her cheek: fool,
     fool—only touch her!

Love: Wrath

He was very much the less attractive of the two: heavyset, part punk, part
    L. L. Bean,
both done ineptly; his look as brutal as the bully's who tormented you in
    second grade.
She was delicate and pretty; what she was suffering may have drawn her
    features finer.
As I went by, he'd just crossed his arms and said, "*You're* the one who's
    fucking us all up!"
He snarled it with a cruelty which made him look all the more a thug, and
    which astonished me,
that he would dare to speak to her like that, be so unafraid of losing her
    unlikely beauty . . .
But still, I knew, love, what he was feeling: the hungering for reason, for
    fair play,
the lust for justice; all the higher systems "Go": the need, the fear, the
    awe, burned away.

Love: The Dance

They're not quite overdressed, just a bit attentively, flashily for seventy-
    five or eighty.
Both wear frosted, frozen, expensive but still delicately balanced and just-
    adhering wigs,
and both have heavy makeup: his could pass for a Miami winter tan, but
    hers goes off the edge—
ice-pink lipstick, badly drawn, thick mascara arching like a ballerina's to-
    ward the brow.
All things considered, she's not built that badly; he has his gut sucked
    nearly neatly in;
their dancing is flamboyant, well rehearsed, old-time ballroom swirls, deft
    romantic dips and bows.
If only they wouldn't contrive to catch our eyes so often, to acknowledge
    with ingratiating grins:
the waltz of life, the waltz of death, and still the heart-work left undone,
    the heavy heart, left undone.

Good Mother: The Métro

Why is he wearing a white confirmation suit—he's only about three—on
  a Thursday morning,
in the Métro station Richelieu-Drouot, and what possibly has he done
  wrong, so wrong,
that his mother should be shrieking at him in a language I don't under-
  stand or even recognize
but whose syllables of raging accusation still pierce and fluster me with an
  intimate anguish?
He *has* done something, too, the way he sits curled up, you know it, the
  way he cries heartfeltly:
it's clearly not the mother's ordinary worries or preoccupations that could
  bring such awful anger . . .
What then? Could he have *shit* himself?—that formulation, "shit yourself,"
  meaning go in your pants:
my mother, I'm sure, never used it, but *someone* did; whoever it was, I
  don't forgive her yet.

Good Mother: The Plane

Bulging overnight bags on both shoulders, in one hand a sack with extra
  diapers, cookies, toys,
in the other a translucent plastic bag, a giant Snoopy grinning with malev-
  olent cuteness through,
"Move, move, move," she keeps saying, nudging the child with her knee,
  "Can't you just move?"
but he, as he's been doing all flight long, obstinately fusses, whines, whim-
  pers, dawdles,
and when she pushes him again lets out a real, really loud, though not a
  really heartfelt howl.
It's midnight, the plane is hours late, for hours she's been reading, singing,
  telling stories,
and now, the gluey California summer air filling up the plane like sweat,
  she finally loses patience,
puts the Snoopy down, an overnight bag, grabs the kid and swats him, to
  the great relief of all.

Good Mother: The Car

At last he's being allowed to play in his mother's car the way he always
        wants to, by himself.
She's brushed some choky pale stuff on her cheeks, smeared the shiny red
        grease on her lips,
made the funny eye-face she makes playing with her lashes, perfume now
        behind her ears,
her wrists, down along her chest, and now she's left him here, smiling at
        him: "Back soon."
He turns the wheel, fast, left and right, clicks the lights, on, off, scrunches
        down to the pedals,
then in not at all a long time here she is again, opening the door, kissing
        him, but, strange,
she puts the makeup on again, exactly as before, no perfume, but the pow-
        der and the lips:
even the fleck of scarlet on a tooth, which with a pinky must be precisely
        fingernailed away.

Good Mother: Out

"I want," he says again, through his tears, in this unfamiliar voice, again,
        "I want, I want,"
not even knowing why he says it now, says it yet again, only knowing that
        he has to say it,
even when she's told him calmly why he can't, then hissed the reasons
        why of course he can't,
then hit him, on the bottom, hard, again, again, and meaning it, so that
        he's crying, sobbing,
but though he sees her growing desperate, though he knows she'll hit him
        again, he says again,
"I want, I want, I want," though he really doesn't care now, doesn't even
        want what might be wanted:
why keep saying it? tears aflow, sobs like painful stones, why must he
        keep on with it?
Does he love her less? Is their relationship ever henceforth to be this?
        Desire, denial, despair?

Good Mother: The Street

He lets the lunch bag fall, he doesn't mean to, really, but there it is, on the
    pavement,
and naturally the little jar of applesauce inside is shattered, naturally the
    paper melts,
and to his horror naturally the gook comes oozing through now, sickly now,
    filthy now; vile.
His fault, his fault, except today it doesn't seem to matter, his mother says
    it doesn't matter,
she's been humming to herself this morning, maybe that's the reason; any-
    way, she bends to it,
uses pieces of the glass to scoop it, carries it to someone's trash: all done—
    she smiles.
Her fingers are still sticky, though; she holds them hanging limply for a
    moment, then,
one by one, she brings them to her pursed lips and with a tiny smack licks
    them clean.

Good Mother: The Bus

Mommy and Daddy are having one of their fights, he can tell by the way
    when Daddy asks something,
Mommy smiles brightly, looking not at Daddy but at him, as though he'd
    asked the question.
He doesn't mind that much at first; it's pleasant being in her arms, being
    smiled at so nicely.
Daddy looks away, out the window, Mommy looks too, out there, with the
    same wide-eyed smile,
but when Daddy looks at her again her smile suddenly is back in *his* face,
    Daddy's somewhere else,
the smile is on *his* forehead—now Mommy kisses it, and finds a smudge
    there to be rubbed away.
What Daddy whispers now *makes* Mommy look, but there's an advertise-
    ment to the left of Daddy's ear,
it's *that* she smiles at this time, a picture of a *dog* . . . How quickly weari-
    some this gets, how saddening.

It was worse than being struck, that tone, that intensity, that abnegating
fervor and furor.

It seemed to open on a kind of limitless irrationality, uncontrollability,
chaos, an abyss,

as though no matter what the cause had been, the occasion that released
this, there might never be

available to them the new antithesis, the new alignment of former senti-
ments which would let it stop.

Sometimes he would feel that both of them were bound in it, as in a force
beyond either of them;

sometimes he thought he felt beneath her rage anxiety, as though she were
frightened by it too.

He wanted to submit, capitulate, atone, if only she would *stop*, but he
could never say, "Please stop,"

because somehow he knew that their connection was as firm in this—
firmer—as in their affection.

Vehicle: Conscience

That moment when the high-wire walker suddenly begins to falter, wob-
ble, sway, arms flailing,
that breathtakingly rapid back-and-forth aligning-realigning of the dis-
placed center of gravity,
weight thrown this way, no, too far; that way, no, too far again, until the
movements themselves
of compensation have their rhythms established so that there's no way
possibly to stop now . . .
that very moment, wheeling back and forth, back and forth, appeal,
repeal, negation,
just before he lets it go and falls to deftly catch himself going by the wire,
somersaulting up,
except for us it never ceases, testing moments of the mind-weight this way,
back and back and forth,
no re-establishing of balance, no place to start again, just this, this force,
this gravity and fear.

Vehicle: Forgetting

The way, playing an instrument, when you botch a passage you have to
stop before you can go on again—
there's a chunk of time you have to wait through, an interval to let the
false notes dissipate,
from consciousness of course, and from the muscles, but it seems also from
the room, the actual air,
the bad try has to leak off into eternity, the volumes of being scrubbed to
let the true resume . . .
So, having loved, and lost, lost everything, the other and the possibility of
other and parts of self,
the heart rushes toward forgetfulness, but never gets there, continuously
attains the opposite instead,
the senses tensed, attending, the conductors of the mind alert, waiting for
the waiting to subside:
when will tedious normality begin again, the old calm silences recur, the
creaking air subside?

Vehicle: Insecurity

The way the voice always, always gives it away, even when you weren't
      aware yourself you felt it,
the tightness in the middle range, the hollow hoarseness lower toward the
      heart that chips, abrades,
shoves against the hindpart of the throat, then takes the throat, then takes
      the voice as well,
as though you'd lost possession of the throat and then the voice or what it
      is that wills the voice
to carry thoughtlessly the thought through tone and word, and then the
      thoughts themselves are lost
and the mind that thought the thoughts begins to lose itself, despairing of
      itself and of its voice,
this infected voice that infects itself with its despair, this voice of terror
      that won't stop,
that lays the trap of doubt, this pit of doubt, this voiceless throat that
      swallows us in doubt.

Vehicle: Indolence

The way it always feels like the early onset of an illness, the viral armies
      mobilizing in the breast,
a restlessness of breath as though the air weren't giving nourishment . . .
      and the way, always, it's not . . .
Gazing into the indifferently insisting morning, trees, sky, great patches
      won't come into focus,
or more exasperatingly come clear, hold a moment, are taken in the moire
      of lapse and inattention.
The way we know that what is being called for is affirmation, the insertion
      of the self into the moral:
this is sin, the very throat of luxury; more than sleep it holds us, more than
      love betrays us . . .
The way we know that if we step across the sluggish stream to act, our
      hovering holiness is saved,
if we submit and sink, we're lost . . . the way, always, we're lost, in these
      irresistible inertias, lost . . .

Vehicle: Circles

It was like simply wanting to give up at last, the saying fifty times a day,
     not quite to yourself,
"I'm tired, so tired of this, of everything," until you'd forgotten somehow
     what you were tired of,
and realized, unavailingly, hopelessly, that saying it meant something else,
     to you, to life,
something closer to the "Help me! Please!" you used to want to cry out,
     aloud, again, to no one,
for no reason, for simply being there, here, baffled by these quantities of
     need and groundless sorrow . . .
How could you have gone past that, only to arrive at this, this about which
     there is nothing whatsoever
you can feel except the certainty of knowing that you're doing what you're
     doing to yourself, but why?
And if you pass this, what will that have meant, what will it have cost to
     accomplish *this* undoing?

Vehicle: Absence

The way, her father dead a day ago, the child goes in his closet, finds her-
     self inside his closet,
finds herself atop the sprawl of emptied shoes, finds herself enveloped in
     the heavy emptied odor,
and breathes it in, that single, mingled gust of hair and sweat and father-
     flesh and father,
breathes it in and tries to hold it, in her body, in her breath, keep it in her
     breath forever . . .
so we, in love, in absence, in an absence so much less than death but still
     shaped by need and loss,
so we too find only what we want in sense, the drive toward sense, the
     hunger for the actual flesh;
so we, too, breathe in, as though to breathe was now itself the end of all,
     as though to scent,
to hold the fading traces of an actual flesh, was all, the hungering senses
     driven toward all . . .

Vehicle: Violence

The way boxers postulate a feeling to label that with which they over-
come the body's vile fears,
its wish to flinch, to flee, break and run . . . they call it anger, pride, the
primal passion to prevail;
the way, before they start, they glare at one another, try to turn themselves
to snarling beasts . . .
so we first make up something in the soul we name and offer credence to—
"meaning," "purpose," "end"—
and then we cast ourselves into the conflict, turn upon our souls, snarl like
snarling beasts . . .
And the way the fighters fight, coolly until strength fails, then desperately,
wildly, as in a dream,
and the way, done, they fall in one another's arms, almost sobbing with
relief, sobbing with relief:
so we contend, so we wish to finish, wish to cry and end, but we never cry,
never end, as in a dream.

III

Le Petit Salvié

for Paul Zweig

1935–1984

1

The summer has gone by both quickly and slowly. It's been a kind of eternity, each day spinning out its endlessness, and yet with every look back, less time is left . . .

So quickly, and so slowly . . . In the tiny elevator of the flat you'd borrowed on the Rue de Pondicherry,
you suddenly put your head against my chest, I thought to show how tired you were, and lost consciousness,
sagging heavily against me, forehead oiled with sweat, eyes ghastly agape . . . so quickly, so slowly.
Quickly the ambulance arrives, mewling at the curb, the disinterested orderlies strap you to their stretcher.
Slowly at the clinic, waiting for the doctors, waiting for the ineffectual treatments to begin.
Slowly through that night, then quickly all the next day, your last day, though no one yet suspects it.
Quickly those remaining hours, quickly the inconsequential tasks and doings of any ordinary afternoon.
Quickly, slowly, those final silences and sittings I so regret now not having taken all of with you.

2

"I don't think we'll make the dance tonight," I mumble mawkishly. "It's
    definitely worse," you whisper.
Ice pack hugged to you, you're breathing fast; when you stop answering
    questions, your eyes close.
You're there, and then you slip away into your meditations, the way, it
    didn't matter where,
in an airport, a café, you could go away into yourself to work, and so we're
    strangely comforted.
It was dusk, late, the softening, sweetening, lingering light of the endless
    Paris evening.
Your room gave on a garden, a perfect breeze washed across your bed, it
    wasn't hard to leave you,
we knew we'd see you again: we kissed you, Vikki kissed you, "Goodbye,
    my friends," you said,
lifting your hand, smiling your old warming smile, then you went into your
    solitude again.

3

We didn't know how ill you were . . . we knew how ill but hid it . . . we
    didn't know how ill you were . . .
Those first days when your fever rose . . . if we'd only made you go into
    the hospital in Brive . . .
Perhaps you could have had another year . . . but the way you'd let death
    touch your life so little,
the way you'd learned to hold your own mortality before you like an un-
    familiar, complex flower . . .
Your stoicism had become so much a part of your identity, your virtue, the
    system of your self-regard;
if we'd insisted now, you might have given in to us, when we didn't,
    weren't we cooperating
with what wasn't just your wish but your true passion never to be dying,
    sooner dead than dying?
You did it, too: composed a way from life directly into death, the ignoble
    scribblings between elided.

4

It must be some body-thing, some species-thing, the way it comes to take
    me from so far,
this grief that tears me so at moments when I least suspect it's there,
    wringing tears from me
I'm not prepared for, had no idea were even there in me, this most un-
    manly gush I almost welcome,
these cries so general yet with such power of their own I'm stunned to
    hear them come from me.
Walking through the street, I cry, talking later to a friend, I try not to but
    I cry again,
working at my desk I'm taken yet again, although, again, I don't want to
    be, not now, not again,
though that doesn't mean I'm ready yet to let you go . . . what it does
    mean I don't think I know,
nor why I'm so ill prepared for this insistence, this diligence with which
    consciousness afflicts us.

5

I imagine you rising to something like heaven: my friend who died last
    year is there to welcome you.
He would know the place by now, he would guide you past the ledges and
    the thorns and terror.
Like a child I am, thinking of you rising in the rosy clouds and being up
    there with him,
being with your guru Baba, too, the three of you, all strong men, all partly
    wild children,
wandering through my comforting child's heaven, doing what you're sup-
    posed to do up there forever.
I tell myself it's silly, all of this, absurd, what we sacrifice in attaining ra-
    tional mind,
but there you are again, glowing, grinning down at me from somewhere
    in the heart of being,
ablaze with wonder and a child's relief that this after all is how astonish-
    ingly it finishes.

6

In my adult mind, I'm reeling, lost—I can't grasp anymore what I even
    think of death.
I don't know even what we hope for: ecstasy? bliss? or just release from
    being, not to suffer anymore.
At the grave, the boring rabbi said that you were going to eternal rest:
    rest? why rest?
Better say we'll be absorbed into the "Thou," better be consumed in light,
    in Pascal's "Fire"!
Or be taken to the Godhead, to be given meaning now, at last, the mean-
    ing we knew eluded us.
God, though, Godhead, Thou, even fire: all that is gone now, gone the
    dark night arguments,
gone the partial answers, the very formulations fail; I grapple for the
    questions as *they* fail.
Are we to be redeemed? When? How? After so much disbelief, will some-
    thing be beyond us to receive us?

7

Redemption is in life, "beyond" unnecessary: it is radically demeaning to
    any possible divinity
to demand that life be solved by yet another life: we're compressed into
    this single span of opportunity
for which our gratitude should categorically be presumed; this is what
    eternity for us consists of,
praise projected from the soul, as love first floods outward to the other
    then back into the self . . .
Yes, yes, I try to bring you to this, too; yes, what is over now is over; yes,
    we offer thanks,
for what you had, for what we all have: this portion of eternity is no dif-
    ferent from eternity,
they both contract, expand, cast up illusion and delusion and all the com-
    fort that we have is love,
praise, the grace not to ask for other than we have . . . yes and yes, but
    this without conviction, too.

8

What if after, though, there is something else, will there be judgment then, will it be retributive,

and if it is, if there is sin, will you have to suffer some hellish match with what your wrongs were?

So much good you did, your work, your many kindnesses, the befriendings and easy generosities.

What sort of evil do we dare imagine we'd have to take into those awful rectifications?

We hurt one another, all of us are helpless in that, with so much vulnerable and mortal to defend.

But that vulnerability, those defenses, our belittling jealousies, resentments, thrusts and spites

are the very image of our frailty: shouldn't our forgiveness for them and our absolution be assumed?

Why would our ultimate identities be burdened with absolutes, imperatives, lost discordant hymns?

9

How ambiguous the triumphs of our time, the releasing of the intellect from myth and magic.

We've gained much, we think, from having torn away corrupted modes of aggrandizement and giantism,

those infected and infecting errors that so long held sway and so bloated our complacencies

that we would willingly inflict even on our own flesh the crippling implications of our metaphysic.

How much we've had to pay, though, and how dearly had to suffer for our liberating dialectics.

The only field still left to us to situate our anguish and uncertainty is in the single heart,

and how it swells, the heart, to bear the cries with which we troubled the startled heavens.

Now we have the air, transparent, and the lucid psyche, and gazing inward, always inward, to the wound.

10

The best evidence I have of you isn't my memory of you, or your work,
    although I treasure both,
and not my love for you which has too much of me in it as subject, but
    the love others bore you,
bear you, especially Vikki, who lived out those last hard years with you,
    the despairs and fears,
the ambivalences and withdrawals, until that final week of fever that
    soaked both your pillows.
Such a moving irony that your last days finally should have seared the
    doubt from both of you.
Sometimes it's hard to tell exactly whom I cry for—you, that last night as
    we left you there,
the way you touched her with such solicitude, or her, the desolation she
    keeps coming to:
*"I've been facing death, touched death, and now I have a ghost I love and
    who loves me."*

11

Genevieve, your precious Gen, doesn't quite know when to cry, or how
    much she's supposed to cry,
or how to understand those moments when it passes, when she's distracted
    into play and laughter
by the other kids or by the adults who themselves don't seem to grasp this
    terrible non-game.
At the cemetery, I'm asked to speak to her, comfort her: never more im-
    possible to move beyond cliché.
We both know we're helplessly embedded in ritual: you wanted her, I
    tell her, to be happy,
that's all, all her life, which she knows, of course, but nods to, as she knows
    what I don't say,
the simplest self-revealing truths, your most awful fear, the brutal fact of
    your mortality:
how horribly it hurt to go from her, how rending not being here to help
    bear this very pain.

12

Nothing better in the world than those days each year with you, your wife,
    my wife, the children,
at your old stone house in the Dordogne, looking over valleys one way,
    chestnut woods the other,
walks, long talks, visits to Lascaux or Les Eyzies, reading, listening to
    each other read.
Our last night, though, I strolled into the moonless fields, it might have
    been a thousand centuries ago,
and something suddenly was with me: just beyond the boundaries of my
    senses presences were threatening,
something out of childhood, mine or humankind's; I felt my fear, familiar,
    unfamiliar, fierce,
might freeze me to the dark, but I looked back—I wasn't here alone, your
    house was there,
the zone of warmth it made was there, you yourself were there, circled in
    the waiting light.

13

I seem to have to make you dead, dead again, to hold you in my mind so
    I can clearly have you,
because unless I do, you aren't dead, you're only living somewhere out of
    sight, I'll find you,
soon enough, no need to hurry, and my mind slips into this other tense,
    other grammar of condition,
in which you're welded to banalities of fact and time, the reality of what
    is done eluding me.
If you're accessible to me, how can you be dead? You are accessible to me,
    therefore . . . something else.
So what I end with is the death of death, but not as it would have been
    elaborated once,
in urgencies of indignation, resignation, faith: I have you neither here, nor
    there, but not not-anywhere:
the soul keeps saying that you might be here, or there—the incessant pas-
    sions of the possible.

Here's where we are: out behind the house in canvas chairs, you're read-
    ing new poems to me,
as you have so often, in your apartment, a park in Paris—anywhere: side-
    walk, restaurant, museum.
You read musically, intensely, with flourishes, convictions: I might be the
    audience in a hall,
and you are unimaginably insecure, you so want me to admire every poem,
    every stanza, every line,
just as I want, need, you, too, to certify, approve, legitimize, all without a
    doubt or reservation,
and which neither of us does, improving everything instead, suggesting
    and correcting and revising,
as we knew, however difficult it was, we had to, in our barely overcome
    but overcome competitiveness.
How I'll miss it, that so tellingly accurate envy sublimated into warmth
    and brothership.

Here's where we are: clearing clumps of shrub and homely brush from
    the corner of your yard,
sawing down a storm-split plum tree, then hacking at the dozens of ma-
    levolently armored maguey:
their roots are frail as flesh and cut as easily, but in the August heat the
    work is draining.
Now you're resting, you're already weak although neither of us will admit
    it to the other.
Two weeks later, you'll be dead, three weeks later, three months, a year,
    I'll be doing this,
writing this, bound into this other labor that you loved so much and that
    we also shared,
still share, somehow always will share now as we shared that sunny late-
    summer afternoon,
children's voices, light; you, pale, leaning on the wall, me tearing at the
    vines and nettles.

16

"A man's life cannot be silent; living is speaking, dying, too, is speaking,"
    so you wrote,
so we would believe, but still, how understand what the finished life could
    have meant to say
about the dying and the death that never end, about potential gone, in-
    spiration unaccomplished,
love left to narrow in the fallacies of recall, eroding down to partial ges-
    ture, partial act?
And we are lessened with it, amazed at how much our self-worth and joy
    were bound into the other.
There are no consolations, no illuminations, nothing of that long-awaited
    flowing toward transcendence.
There is, though, compensation, the simple certainty of having touched
    and having been touched.
The silence and the speaking come together, grief and gladness come to-
    gether, the disparates fuse.

17

Where are we now? Nowhere, anywhere, the two of us, the four of us,
    fifty of us at a *fête*.
Islands of relationship, friends and friends, the sweet, normal, stolid ma-
    trix of the merely human,
the circles of community that intersect within us, hold us, touch us always
    with their presence,
even as, today, mourning, grief, themselves becoming memory, there still
    is that within us which endures,
not in possession of the single soul in solitude, but in the covenants of
    affection we embody,
the way an empty house embodies elemental presences, and the way, at-
    tentive, we can sense them.
Breath held, heart held, body stilled, we attend, and they are there, cove-
    nant, elemental presence,
and the voice, in the lightest footfall, the eternal wind, leaf and earth, the
    constant voice.

"The immortalities of the moment spin and expand; they seem to have no
limits, yet time passes.

These last days here are bizarrely compressed, busy, and yet full of sup-
pressed farewells . . ."

The hilly land you loved, lucerne and willow, the fields of butterfly and
wasp and flower.

Farewell the crumbling house, barely held together by your ministrations,
the shed, the pond.

Farewell your dumb French farmer's hat, your pads of yellow paper, your
joyful, headlong scrawl.

The coolness of the woods, the swallow's swoop and whistle, the confident
call of the owl at night.

Scents of dawn, the softening all-night fire, char, ash, warm embers in the
early morning chill.

The moment holds, you move across the path and go, the light lifts, breaks:
goodbye, my friend, farewell.